Traditional Black Music

Children's Songs

Jerry Silverman

CHELSEA HOUSE PUBLISHERS

New York   Philadelphia

On the cover Accompanying himself on guitar, a young balladeer sings a traditional children's song.

Chelsea House Publishers

Editor-in-Chief Richard S. Papale
Executive Managing Editor Karyn Gullen Browne
Copy Chief Philip Koslow
Picture Editor Adrian G. Allen
Art Director Nora Wertz
Manufacturing Director Gerald Levine
Production Coordinator Marie Claire Cebrián-Ume

Staff for Children's Songs

Text Editor Marian W. Taylor
Picture Researcher Sandy Jones
Book Layout Jesse Cohen, Robert Yaffe

First Printing
1 3 5 7 9 8 6 4 2

Library of Congress Cataloging-in-Publication Data

Children's Songs/[compiled by]Jerry Silverman.
  1 score. — (Traditional Black Music)
  For voice and piano; includes chord symbols.
  Includes index.

Summary: Thirty songs with an Afro-American source, including One
  More River, The Gray Goose, and Hush Little Children.
  0-7910-1831-8   0-7910-1847-4 (pbk.)
1. Children songs—United States. 2. Afro-American children—
Music. [1. Songs. 2. Afro-Americans—Music.] I. Silverman, Jerry.
II. Series.   92-15472
M1992.C515 1993   CIP AC M

PICTURE CREDITS

The Bettmann Archive: pp. 25, 35, 47, 55, 59; FPG International: p. 63; Gannett Suburban Newspapers/Wendy Vissar: p. 5; Copyright Chester Higgins, Jr.: cover; Copyright © 1992 by Donna Mussenden Van Der Zee: p. 13; Shirley Zeiberg: pp. 7, 21, 43, 49

CONTENTS

Author's Preface

Children sing about things they have seen and done themselves, and they sing about things that happened before their birth, about the experiences of their ancestors. Many of the "play songs" sung by today's black American children are rooted in the call-and-response songs of long-ago Africa. Filtered through blacks' collective experience of slavery and its dark aftermath, the songs' harsh realities have gentled as one generation passed them on to the next. In slavery days, for example, a runaway had one special fear as he or she dashed through the night: "paterollers," vengeful slave hunters who administered fearful punishment to those they caught. In "Run, Chillen, Run," however, flight from the pateroller becomes a game, and the worst fate a participant can suffer is loss of a "Sunday shoe."

In another type of transformation, black children's music often interposes animals—Brother Rabbit, Mr. Frog, Miss Mouse, and others—for people. Animals often show up in lullabies, probably the strongest musical bond between parent and child. With love, the older person offers anything the younger might wish for, from "all the pretty little horses" to "a billy goat."

Parents expose their children to another trove of intriguing characters and stories by sending them to Sunday school. In black children's songs, such biblical heroes and villains as Noah, Jonah and the whale, David and Goliath, and the angel Gabriel come alive. Just as important as a song's subject matter, of course, is the music itself. The songs of black children contain all the melodic, rhythmic, harmonic, and stylistic ingredients of "grown-up" black music. Syncopation and blue notes, slurs and slides, repetition and improvisation—they are all here.

Children sing—in their own terms—of love and courting, work and play, religion and death. What, then, is a children's song—a black children's song? It is a musical look at the child's world, blending gentle fantasy and down-to-earth reality, physical movement and quiet repose, with an appealing melody and an engaging performance style. It is, in short, black music.

Jerry Silverman

The Contribution of Blacks to American Art and Culture

Kenneth B. Clark

Historical and contemporary social inequalities have obscured the major contribution of American blacks to American culture. The historical reality of slavery and the combined racial isolation, segregation, and sustained educational inferiority have had deleterious effects. As related pervasive social problems determine and influence the art that any group can not only experience, but also, ironically, the extent to which they can eventually contribute to the society as a whole, this tenet is even more visible when assessing the contributions made by African Americans.

All aspects of the arts have been pursued by black Americans, but music provides a special insight into the persistent and inescapable social forces to which black Americans have been subjected. One can speculate that in their preslavery patterns of life in Africa, blacks used rhythm, melody, and lyrics to hold on to reality, hope, and the acceptance of life. Later, in America, music helped blacks endure the cruelties of slavery. Spirituals and gospel music provided a medium for both communion and communication. As the black experience in America became more complex, so too did black music, which has grown and ramified, dramatically affecting the development of American music in general. The result is that today, more than ever before, black music provides a powerful lens through which we may view the history of black Americans in a new and revealing way.

Members of an urban boys' choir join their voices in a spirited rendition of "Rise and Shine."

Of all the animals, the rabbit turns up most often in black folk song and story. It is no wonder that slaves regarded him with respect and envy; fleet-footed and wily, Mr. Rabbit embodies the qualities needed for survival—or escape. In this song, the admirable creature demonstrates yet another skill: he always gets the last word, even in conversation with the "dear Lord."

MISTER RABBIT

"Mis - ter Rab - bit, Mis - ter Rab - bit, your tail's might - y white."

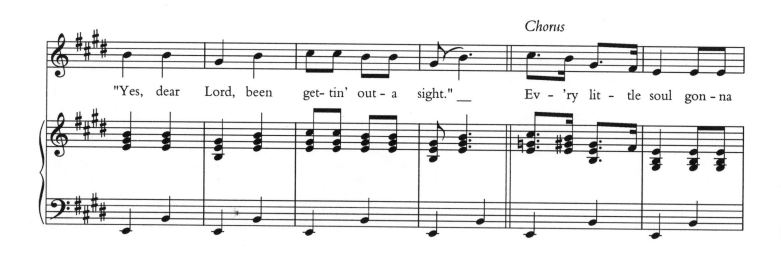

"Yes, dear Lord, been get - tin' out - a sight." __ Ev - 'ry lit - tle soul gon - na

shine, shine. __ Ev - 'ry lit - tle soul gon - na shine a - long.

"Mister Rabbit, Mister Rabbit, your coat's mighty grey."
"Yes, dear Lord, been out all day." *Chorus*

"Mister Rabbit, Mister Rabbit, your ears mighty long."
"Yes, dear Lord, been put on wrong." *Chorus*

"Mister Rabbit, Mister Rabbit, your ears mighty thin."
"Yes, dear Lord, been splittin' the wind." *Chorus*

The always intriguing "Mr. Rabbit"—in this case, a lop-eared backyard bunny—enchants a pair of suburban youngsters.

This is a classic pre–Civil War lullaby that has lived on to our own time. In the song, a black woman rocks her master's child to sleep as her own baby lies alone "way down yonder in the meadow." The mother softly promises the white infant "pretty little horses," but her heart aches for her own "poor little lambie," and she worries about "bees and butterflies pecking out its eyes." Because time has softened the sadness of "All the Pretty Little Horses," today's mother can sing it with a gentle smile. Her children will love it.

ALL THE PRETTY LITTLE HORSES

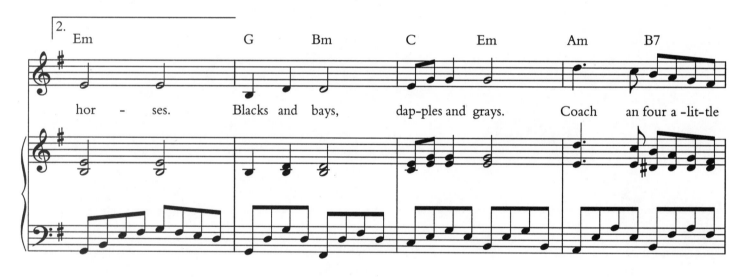

Hush-a-bye, don't you cry,
Go to sleepy, little baby.
Way down yonder in the meadow
Lies a poor little lambie.

The bees and the butterflies pecking out its eyes,
The poor little thing cried, "Mammy."
Hush-a-bye, don't you cry,
Go to sleepy, little baby.

Children are intrigued by the image of Noah's animals marching aboard his Ark "by twosy, twosy." They often use it in their drawings and always enjoy singing about it. Sparking this musical retelling is an irresistible African-American syncopation that commands all the world to "rise and shine and give God the glory, glory!" The song never fails to trigger rhythmic hand-clapping and boisterous foot-stomping by everyone within earshot.

RISE AND SHINE

The Lord said, "Noah, there's gonna be a floody, floody."
The Lord said, "Noah, there's gonna be a floody, floody.
Get your children out of the muddy, muddy!"
Children of the Lord.

Noah, he built him, he built him an arky, arky,
Noah, he built him, he built him an arky, arky.
Made it out of hickory barky, barky.
Children of the Lord.

The animals, they came, they came by twosy, twosy,
The animals, they came, they came by twosy, twosy,
Elephants and kangaroosy, roosy.
Children of the Lord.

It rained and rained for forty daysy, daysy,
It rained and rained for forty daysy, daysy,
Drove those animals nearly crazy, crazy.
Children of the Lord.

Repeat Verse One

Here is a wonderfully mixed-up children's song. First, we have the beloved Noah's Ark story combined with traditional numerical rhyming verses. Then Noah loads up his passengers and they all float around until they land on Mount Ararat—just as the chorus crosses the River Jordan into the Promised Land. This happy jumble of biblical tales is wrapped in a particularly bouncy melody in six-eight time.

ONE MORE RIVER

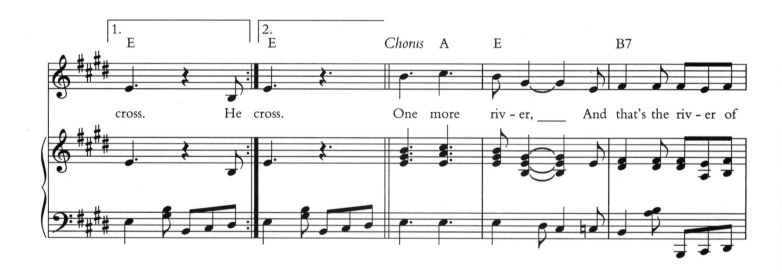

The animals went in one by one...
The elephant chewing a caraway bun...

The animals went in two by two...
The rhinoceros and the kangaroo...

The animals went in three by three...
The bear, the flea and the bumble bee...

The animals went in four by four...
Old Noah got mad and hollered for more...

The animals went in five by five...
With Saratoga trunks they did arrive...

The animals went in six by six...
The hyena laughed at the monkey's tricks...

The animals went in seven by seven...
Said the ant to the elephant, "Who are you a-shovin'?"

The animals went in eight by eight...
They came with a rush 'cause 'twas so late...

The animals went in nine by nine...
Old Noah shouted, "Cut that line!"

The animals went in ten by ten...
The Ark she blew her whistle then...

And then the voyage did begin...
Old Noah pulled the gang-plank in...

They never knew where they were at...
Till the old Ark bumped on Ararat...

A Harlem youth introduces two special friends. Animals and children seem to belong together, both in real life and in such rollicking songs as "One More River."

This is what might be termed a Sunday school song. After studying their Bible lessons, the children belt out verse after verse about their favorite characters. Youngsters enjoy making up new stanzas of their own: Moses and Pharaoh, Samson and Delilah, and Joseph and his Coat of Many Colors might be suggested as subjects.

WHO DID SWALLOW JONAH?

Who did, who did, who did, who did, Who did swal - low Jo, Jo, Jo - nah?

Who did, who did, who did, who did, Who did swal - low Jo, Jo, Jo - nah?

Who did, who did, who did, who did, who did swal-low Jo, Jo, Jo-nah? Who did swal-low Jo - nah?

Who did swal-low Jo - nah? Who did swal-low Jo - nah down?

The whale did, whale did, whale did, whale did, } (3 times)
The whale did swallow Jo-Jo-Jonah
The whale did swallow Jonah, the whale did swallow Jonah
The whale did swallow Jonah - up!

Shadrack, Shadrack, Shadrack, Shadrack, } (3 times)
Shadrack, Meshak, Abindigo
Shadrack, Meshak, Abindi - Shadrack, Meshak, Abindi,
Shadrack, Meshak, Abindigo!

Noah, Noah, Noah, Noah, } (3 times)
Noah in the ark, ark, arky
Noah in the arky, Noah in the arky,
Noah in the arky - bailed!

Daniel, Daniel, Daniel, Daniel, } (3 times)
Daniel in the li-li-lion
Daniel in the lion, Daniel in the lion,
Daniel in the lion's den!

David, David, David, David, } (3 times)
David killed Goli-li-liath
David killed Goliath, David killed Goliath,
David killed Goliath - dead!

Gabriel, Gabriel, Gabriel, Gabriel,
Gabriel, blow your trum, trum, trumpet } (3 times)
Gabriel, blow your trumpet - Gabriel, blow your trumpet,
Gabriel, blow your trumpet loud!

A parable in modern dress, this humorous look at the biblical rich man and the Kingdom of God is enlivened by mock-Latin rhyming words. After endless repetition, once-meaningful phrases often turn into nonsense syllables, which have always captivated children. No "lost meanings" need be looked for here. Just enjoy the sounds!

THE RICH MAN AND THE POOR MAN

There was a rich man, and he lived in Je - ru - sa - lem,

Glo - ry Hal - le - lu - jah hi - ro - je - rum. He wore a silk hat and his

coat was ve - ry spru - ci - um, Glo - ry Hal - le - lu - jah hi - ro - je - rum.

And at his gate there sat a human wreckium,
Glory Hallelujah, hirojerum
He wore a bowler hat and the rim was round his neckium,
Glory Hallelujah, hirojerum *Chorus*

The poor man asked for a piece of bread and cheesium,
Glory Hallelujah, hirojerum
The rich man replied, "I'll call for a policium,"
Glory Hallelujah, hirojerum *Chorus*

The poor man died, and his soul went to Heavium,
Glory Hallelujah, hirojerum
He danced with the angels 'til a quarter past elevium,
Glory Hallelujah, hirojerum *Chorus*

The rich man died, but he didn't fare so wellium,
Glory Hallelujah, hirojerum
He couldn't get to Heaven, so he had to go to Hellium,
Glory Hallelujah, hirojerum *Chorus*

The devil said, "This is no hotelium,"
Glory Hallelujah, hirojerum
"It's just a very common, very ordinary Hellium,"
Glory Hallelujah, hirojerum *Chorus*

The moral of this story is: Riches are no jokium,
Glory Hallelujah, hirojerum
We'll all go to Heaven, 'cause we're all stony-brokium,
Glory Hallelujah, hirojerum *Chorus*

Huddie ("Leadbelly") Ledbetter, one of America's greatest blues singers, also sang work songs, spirituals, and children's songs. He recalled this one from the days when he was in a Louisiana grade school in the 1890s. The boys played ball during recess, he said, but when the girls started playing ring games such as "Ha-ha Thisaway"—which sometimes involved kissing—the ball games were quickly forgotten.

HA-HA THISAWAY

Ha - ha this - a - way, Ha - ha that - a - way, Ha - ha

this - a - way Then, oh, then. When I was a lit - tle boy,

lit - tle boy, lit - tle boy, When I was a lit - tle boy, Twelve years old,

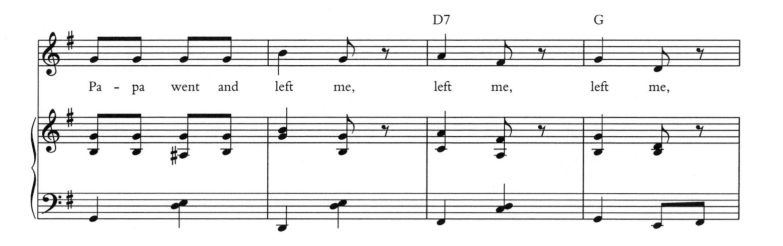

Pa – pa went and left me, left me, left me,

Pa – pa went and left me, save my soul.

to Chorus

Mama come and got me,
Got me, got me,
Mama come and got me,
Save my soul.
Mama didn't whip me,
Whip me, whip me,
Mama didn't whip me,
I been told. *Chorus*

I went to school,
To school, to school,
I went to school,
Save my soul.
Teacher didn't whip me,
Whip me, whip me,
Teacher didn't whip me,
I been told. *Chorus*

Learned my lesson,
Lesson, lesson,
Learned my lesson,
Save my soul.
Wasn't that a blessin',
Blessin', blessin',
Wasn't that a blessin',
I been told. *Chorus*

Liked my teacher,
Teacher, teacher,
Liked my teacher,
Save my soul.
Prayed like a preacher,
Preacher, preacher,
Prayed like a preacher,
I been told. *Chorus*

Sometimes known as "Three Mockingbirds," this song accompanies a Mississippi children's "ring" game—one that, as its name implies, is played in a circle. To begin the game, one player "steals" a partner, then hops around the ring with him or her as other players sing. This loosely structured piece is related to the work song, a chantlike cadence sung by laborers or chain gangs to help make their hard, monotonous efforts bearable.

JANE, JANE

Hey, hey, _____ Jane, Jane, My Lord - y Lord,

Jane, Jane. I'm _____ a gon - na buy, Jane, Jane, Three

mock - ing - birds, Jane, Jane. One _____ a - for to whis - tle

Jane, Jane, One _____ a-for to sing, Jane, Jane, One _____ a-for to do, Jane, Jane, Most an-y lit-tle thing, Jane, Jane.

Each verse begins with the first 12 measures of verse one.

Three hunting dogs,
One a-for to run,
One a-for to shout,
One to talk to,
When I go out.

Three muley cows,
One a-for to milk,
One to plough my corn,
One for to pray,
On Christmas morn.

Three little bluebirds,
One a-for to weep,
One for to mourn,
One for to grieve,
When I am gone.

(Repeat first verse)

Southern children join hands and sing as they play a traditional "ring game."

Abraham Lincoln probably first heard this song when he was a young Illinois lawyer. His supporters sang it in the 1860 presidential election, but they changed the words to "Old Abe Lincoln came out of the wilderness, down in Illinois." Lincoln counted the original version among his favorite songs—and blacks counted Lincoln among their personal heroes. As one former slave put it at the close of the Civil War: "The children of Israel was in bondage one time, and God sent Moses to 'liver them. Well, I s'pose that God sent Abe Lincoln to 'liver us." Perhaps Lincoln's popularity with blacks explains the long-term attraction of "Hoosen Johnny" for black youngsters.

HOOSEN JOHNNY

The lit-tle black bull came down the mead-ow, Hoo-sen John-ny,

Hoo-sen John-ny. The lit-tle black bull came down the mead-ow long time a-

go. Long time a-go, long time a-go. The

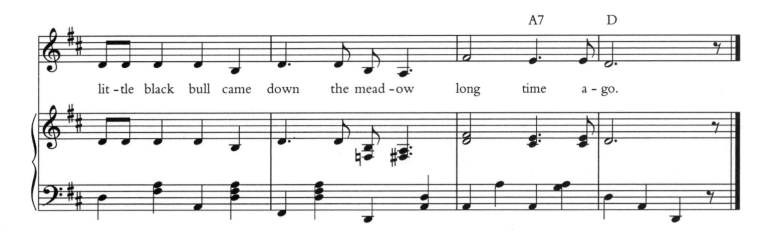

lit -tle black bull came down the mead -ow long time a - go.

First he paw and then he beller,
  Hoosen Johnny, Hoosen Johnny.
First he paw and then he beller,
  Long time ago. *Chorus*

He whet his horn on a white oak saplin',
  Hoosen Johnny, Hoosen Johnny.
He whet his horn on a white oak saplin',
  Long time ago. *Chorus*

He shake his tail, he jar the river,
  Hoosen Johnny, Hoosen Johnny.
He shake his tail, he jar the river,
  Long time ago. *Chorus*

He paw the dirt in the heifers' faces,
  Hoosen Johnny, Hoosen Johnny.
He paw the dirt in the heifers' faces,
  Long time ago. *Chorus*

Always on the lookout for new material, folklorist Harold Courlander took a journey through rural Alabama in 1950. Not far from the Mississippi border, he discovered Lilly's Chapel School, a one-room academy for the children of local black farmers. When Courlander asked the the pupils to sing a few of their favorite songs, they started with this one.

HEY BOB-A-NEEDLE

Hey bob - a - nee - dle, bob - a - nee - dle, bob - a - nee - dle, bob - a,

Hey bob - a - nee - dle, bob - a - nee - dle, bob - a - nee - dle, bob - a,

Hey bob - a - nee - dle, bob - a - nee - dle, bob - a - nee - dle, bob - a,

Hey bob – a – nee – dle, bob – a – nee – dle, bob – a – nee – dle, bob – a,

Hey bob, *(clap)*   Hey bob. *(clap)*

Schoolhouses such as this one-room academy in backwoods Georgia (photographed in 1941) have helped black children's songs live from one generation to the next.

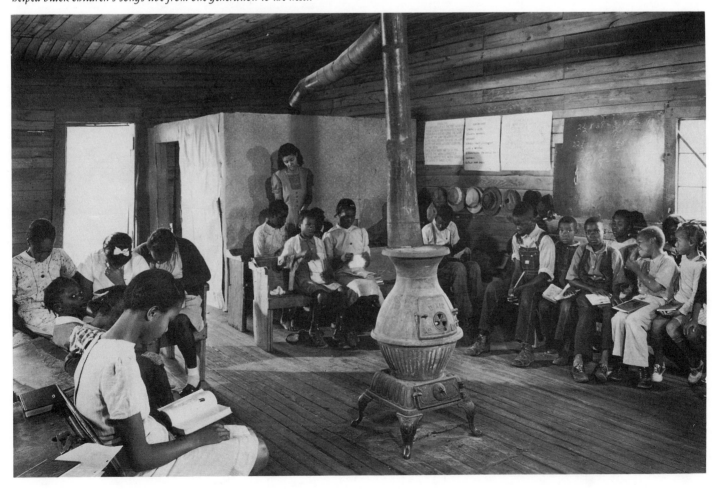

Here is another offering from the children at Lilly's school. Folk songs have always had a mysterious life of their own: as they move from one generation to the next, they also travel around the country, often reappearing far from their birthplaces. The author first heard Alabama's "Miss Mary Mack" from his five-year-old son, David, who had learned it in his kindergarten class in Hastings-on-Hudson, New York.

MISS MARY MACK

Miss Ma - ry Mack, Mack, Mack, All dressed in

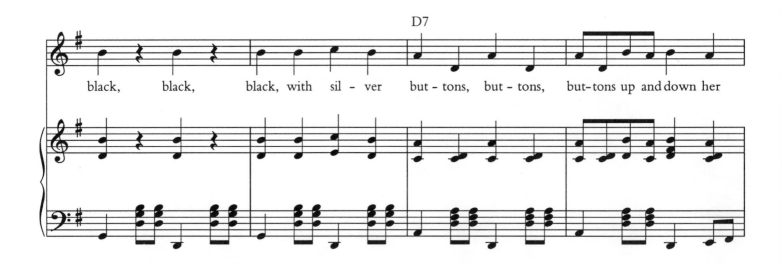

black, black, black, with sil - ver but - tons, but - tons, but-tons up and down her

back, back, back. Well, I love cof- fee, cof- fee, cof- fee, And I love

I went to the river, river, river,
And I couldn't get across, 'cross, 'cross,
And I paid five dollars, dollars, dollars,
For the old grey horse, horse, horse.

And the horse wouldn't pull, pull, pull,
I swapped him for a bull, bull, bull,
And the bull wouldn't holler, holler, holler,
I swapped him for a dollar, dollar, dollar.

And the dollar wouldn't spend, spend, spend,
I put it in the grass, grass, grass,
And the grass wouldn't grow, grow, grow,
I got my hoe, hoe, hoe.

And the hoe wouldn't chop, chop, chop,
I took it to the shop, shop, shop,
And the shop made money, money, money,
Like the bees made honey, honey, honey.

See that yonder, yonder, yonder,
In the jay-bird town, town, town,
Where the women gotta work, work, work,
Till the sun goes down, down, down.

Well, I eat my meat, meat, meat,
And I gnaw my bone, bone, bone,
Well, good-bye honey, honey, honey,
I'm going on home.

This "game song" (words and music that accompany specific movements) comes from the black community at John's Island, South Carolina. To play "Old Lady," participants line up with their feet a few inches apart. As they start to sing, they tap their feet: left, right, left, right, *right*. On the last tap, each player moves slightly to the right. The last tap then becomes the first tap of the second sequence: right, left, right, left, *left*. Following the same pattern, the players move slightly to the left on the last tap. These alternating patterns continue to the end of the song. Children should place their hands on whichever part of the body—head, shoulder, and so on—they are singing about.

OLD LADY COME FROM BOOSTER

Old la - dy come from Boos - ter, she had two hens _ and a roos - ter. The

roos-ter died, _ the old la-dy cried, She could-n't get eggs like she used to. Oh, ma, _ you look so,

Oh, pa, _ you look so, Who's been here since I been gone? Two lit - tle boys with the blue caps on.

Hang them on the hick-'ry stick.   Ran-ky tan-ky, but-ton my shoes,   Buf - fa-lo boy gon-na tell me the news.

Repeat as necessary.

Pain   in my head, __ Ran - ky tan - ky.
   shoul-der, _
   hands, _
   thighs, _
   knees, _
   legs, __
   foot, __

(D)   Am   *twice*

Pain   all   o-ver me,   ran - ky tan - ky.

This game song is the work of Mable Hillery, a member of the Georgia Sea Island Singers who taught music to public school children in New York City's Harlem in the 1970s. Hillery, who specialized in folk songs, blues, and spirituals, created "Walk Along" to introduce traditional African-American music and games to her urban pupils.

Game Directions

1. There must be an even number of boys and girls; girls form a line, standing side by side. Boys do the same, opposite the girls.

Girls XX XX XX

Boys XX XX XX

2. Each player becomes the partner of the person next to her or him.

3. Turning to face one another, partners do a clap-cross-clap pattern four times while chanting the first two lines of the verse.

4. During the last two lines of each verse, players do the "Walk Along."

5. Walk Along Pattern:

a.) Girls' and boys' lines turn to face each other.
b.) Girl partners form arches by joining left and right hands.
c.) Boy partners join hands; girls walk forward and go under the arch directly in front of them.
d.) All players drop hands and face each other, forming two parallel lines.
e.) Boys form arches by joining left and right hands; girl partners go under the arch directly in front of them.
f.) Each group will be back in its original place by the end of the verse.

6. The game is repeated with varying body movements preceding the "Walk Along."

a.) Players clap their hands during the first two lines.
b.) Players snap their fingers during the first two lines.
c.) Players shake their legs in an alternating pattern.
d.) Players shake their hips from side to side four times.
e.) Players shake their arms in an alternating pattern.

7. Players walk around in a circle and clap while chanting the final verse.

WALK ALONG

Come on, Earl, and hush your talk - ing, Let's join hands and we'll go walk - ing.

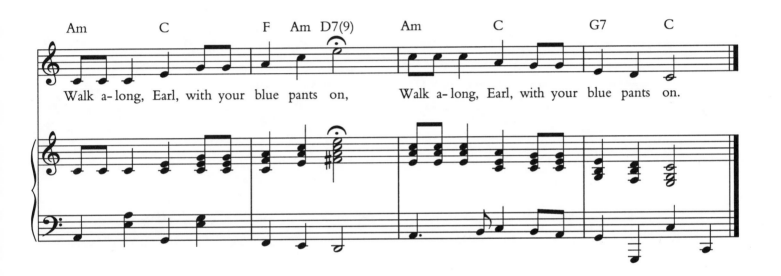

Walk a-long, Earl, with your blue pants on, Walk a-long, Earl, with your blue pants on.

Come on, Judy, and hush your talking,
Let's clap hands and we'll go walking.
Walk along, Judy, with your red dress on,
Walk along, Judy, with your red dress on.

Come on, Janet, and hush your talking,
Let's snap our fingers and we'll go walking.
Walk along, Janet, with your yellow dress on,
Walk along, Janet, with your yellow dress on.

Come on, Michael, and hush your talking,
Let's shake out our legs and we'll go walking.
Walk along, Michael, with your red hat on,
Walk along, Michael, with your red hat on.

Come on, Peaches, and hush your talking,
Let's shake our hips and we'll go walking.
Walk along, Peaches, with your green socks on,
Walk along, Peaches, with your green socks on.

Come on, Tony, and hush your talking,
Let's shake our arms and we'll go walking.
Walk along, Tony, with your black tie on,
Walk along, Tony, with your black tie on.

Sung to last 2 measures, repeated.

Walk along, Earl with your blue pants on.
Walk along, Judy, with your red dress on.
Walk along, Janet, with your yellow dress on.
Walk along, Michael, with your red hat on.
Walk along, Peaches, with your green socks on.
Walk along, Tony, with your black tie on.

This is a variant of "Froggie Went a-Courting," one of the oldest and best-loved songs in the English language. A favorite of all children, "King Kong Kitchie" tells the story of brave Mr. Frog's courtship of the lovely Miss Mouse.

KING KONG KITCHIE KITCHIE KI-ME-O

Frog went a court - ing and he did ride, King kong kit-chie kit-chie ki - me - o, With a

sword and a pis - tol by his side, King kong kit-chie kit-chie ki - me - o.

Chorus
Ki - mo ke - mo ki - mo kee, Way down yon-der in a hol - low tree. An

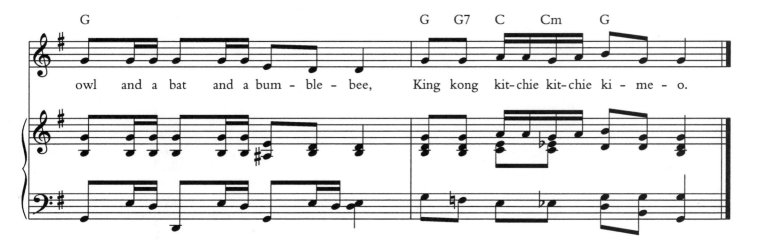

He rode till he came to Miss Mouse's door,
King kong kitchie kitchie ki-me-o,
And there he knelt upon the floor,
King kong kitchie kitchie ki-me-o. *Chorus*

similarly

He took Miss Mouse up on his knee . . .
And he said, "Little mouse will you marry me?" . . . *Chorus*

Miss Mouse had suitors three or four . . .
And there they came right in the door . . . *Chorus*

They grabbed Mr. Frog and began to fight . . .
In that hollow tree t'was a terrible night . . . *Chorus*

Mr. Frog hurled the suitors to the floor . . .
With his sword and his pistol he killed all four . . . *Chorus*

They went to the parson the very next day . . .
And left on their honeymoon right away . . . *Chorus*

Now they live far off in a hollow tree . . .
Where they now have wealth and children three . . . *Chorus*

Rose Thompson, an official of the Farm Security Administration in rural Georgia, found this song and its story in the 1930s. Typical of American blacks' strong oral tradition, the tale can be traced back to its African heritage: conversations with evil spirits are possible, and music—in this case, the "flu-to-to," or flute—has the power to overcome those spirits. Here is part of the story Thompson discovered:

One time there was a little boy going down the road singing a little lonesome song that sounded sort of pitiful like this: "Went down to Gran'ma's ground pea patch . . ." Then the little boy met the devil right in the bend of the road. The devil stopped dead in his tracks and he said, "Where have you been, boy?" The little boy was so scared he could hardly talk but he knew he was obliged to be polite to the devil so he said, sort of pitiful, "Been down to Gran'ma's ground pea patch." "For what?" asked the devil. And the little boy said, "To get my little flu-to-to." "For what?" said the devil like he is getting out of patience with the little boy. The boy was so scared that his legs gave away under him, but he said, "To blow to my little sister now, flu-to to Aunt Nancy, flu-to to Aunt Jane." Then the little boy shut his eyes and hoped that the devil would be gone when he opened them. But about that time the devil reached down and caught the poor little boy and crammed him into a sack and threw the sack over his back and hurried home. When he got there, he locked the litle boy up in a room and left him right by himself. Then the devil went off about his business. After a while, the devil's wife heard the little boy singing that sad little old song and she cracked open the door and said, "What is that you are singing about going to gran'ma's pea patch? Let me hear you sing it then." And the little boy said, "I can sing it a heap better if you will open the door a little wider so I can get some air." Then the devil's wife opened the door a little wider and the little boy sang the song. And, Lawd bless my soul, that little boy sang that song so pitiful that the devil's wife nearly about cried her eyes plumb out. She cried so hard that she didn't see the little boy when he slipped out through the crack in the door and went running down that road.

FLU-TO-TO

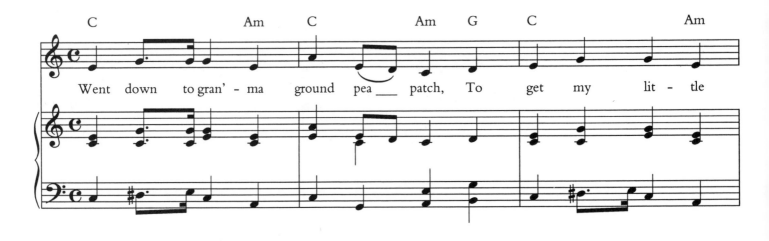

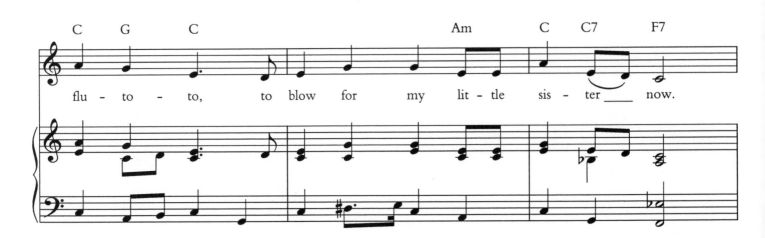

Flu – to, Aunt Nan – cy, flu – to, Aunt Jane.

A young Georgia musician prepares to supply the rhythm for a group sing-a-long.

Here is another song about Brother Rabbit, hero of so many black folk tales and songs. In one popular tale, the rabbits, tired of being chased, ask the dogs to please leave them alone. The dogs agree, and Brer Rabbit then accepts Brer Dog's invitation to dinner at his house. But on the way, Brer Rabbit hears dogs barking and stops in his tracks. "Aw come on, Brer Rabbit, you always gittin' scared for nothin'," says Brer Dog. "Ah hears dogs barkin', Brer Dog," says Rabbit. "S'posin' it is, it don't make no difference," says Brer Dog. "Ain't we done passed a law dogs run no mo' rabbits?" Rabbit scratch his ear and say, "Yeah, but some o' dese fool dogs ain't got no better sense than to run all over dat law and break it up. De rabbit didn't go to school much and he didn't learn much, but he know to run every time de bush shake." So he raced on home without breakin' another breath wid de dog.

BROTHER RABBIT

D.C. al Fine

This is a Georgia "play-party" song, a term used by folklorists to describe music that calls for action or dancing. In "Sandy Land," the children take partners and join hands in a circle. They all take four steps into the center, lifting their hands, then four steps back, dropping hands. They repeat these movements. Next, partners hook elbows with each other and turn around in place. Finally, all join hands and skip in a circle.

SANDY LAND

Raise big 'taters in sandy land,
Raise big 'taters in sandy land,
Raise big 'taters in sandy land,
If you can't dig 'em, I guess I can.

Hop, come along, my pretty little miss,
Hop, come along, my honey,
Hop, come along, my pretty little miss,
I won't be home till Sunday.

This song dates from slavery, when the villain was not "Aunt Kate" but "the white folks." Frederick Douglass, the former slave who became a great abolitionist, writer, and orator, noted that "once in a while among a mass of nonsense and wild frolic, a sharp hit was given to the meanness of slaveholders." Douglass recalled slaves singing these lyrics: "We peel de meat / Dey gib us de skin / And dat's de way / Dey take us in / We skim de pot / Dey gib us de liquor / And say dat's good enough for nigger."

"Old Aunt Kate" shows how time can change meaning: here, a bitter song of protest has become a humorous comment on sneaky people.

OLD AUNT KATE

Like rabbits, trains frequently appear in black lore and song. Trains, of course, represent departure and freedom, precious concepts to an enslaved people.

Children love to hear their own names in a "real" song; when they sing this one, they may substitute themselves for "Miss Julie Ann."

MISS JULIE ANN JOHNSON

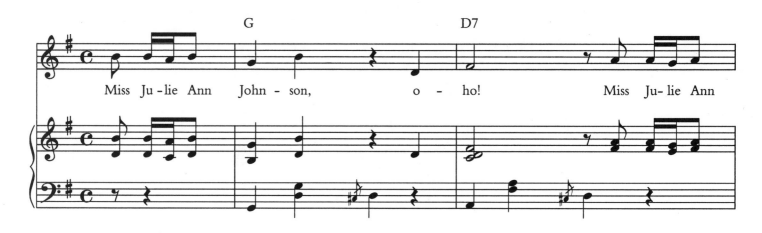

Oh, where's my Julie? o-ho!	Going to catch that train, boys, o-ho!	Going to hug my Julie, o-ho!
Oh, where's my Julie? o-ho!	Going to catch that train, boys, o-ho!	Going to hug my Julie, o-ho!
She's gone to Dallas, o-ho!	Going to find my Julie, o-ho!	Miss Julie Ann Johnson, o-ho!
She's gone to Dallas, o-ho!	Going to find my Julie, o-ho!	Miss Julie Ann Johnson, o-ho!

The image of a "glory train," loaded up with true believers and ready to leave for heaven, crops up regularly in black traditional music. "The Train Is a-Coming" is less specifically religious than some of these songs, but its message is clear: get religion ("your ticket") and get on board before it is too late; the train is even now "a-leaving."

THE TRAIN IS A-COMING

Better get your ticket, oh, yes,
Better get your ticket, oh, yes.
Better get your ticket, better get your ticket,
Better get your ticket, oh, yes.

similarly
Room for a-many more, oh, yes...

Train is a-leaving, oh, yes...

I'm on my way to glory, oh yes...

This action song has always appealed to children, especially the very young. Parents and teachers should encourage their youngsters to make all the movements indicated ("walk," "hop," "skip," and so on.) and then to make up and perform their own variations.

JIM ALONG JOSIE

Chorus

Hey Jim a - long, __ Jim a- long Jo - sie, Hey Jim a- long, __ Jim a- long Jo.

Hey Jim a- long, __ Jim a-long Jo - sie, Hey Jim a-long, __ Jim a- long Jo.

Fine

Verse

Walk Jim a - long, __ Jim a-long Jo - sie, Walk Jim a - long, __ Jim a- long Jo.

Walk Jim a - long, __ Jim a - long Jo - sie, Walk Jim a-long, _ Jim a-long Jo.

D.C.
al Fine

Hop Jim a-long, Jim-along Josie,
Hop Jim a-long, Jim-along Jo.
Hop Jim a-long, Jim-along Josie,
Hop Jim a-long, Jim-along Jo. *Chorus*

similarly

Skip . . .

Jump . . .

Swing . . .

Bounce . . .

Crawl . . .

As their classmates look on with delighted laughter, a girl and boy perform their roles in an "action song."

Here is a contribution from the island of Nassau in the Bahamas. Like many Caribbean children's songs, "The Wind Blow East" deals with a hurricane; this one blew two boats, the *Sunshine* and the *Setting Star*, "right down in town," and followed that up with a flood. Other songs in this vein include "Deep Blue Sea" ("It was Willie what got drownded in the deep blue sea"), "Mighty Day" ("I remember one September, storm winds struck the town"), and "Run Come See" ("When the first wave struck the *Pretoria*").

THE WIND BLOW EAST

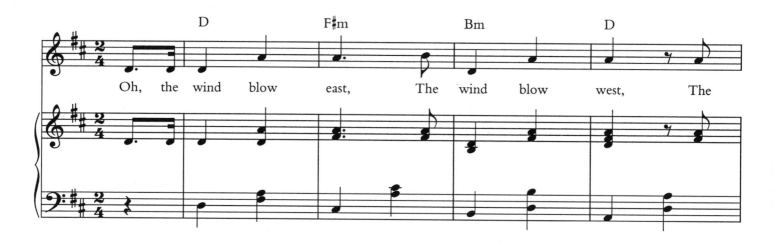

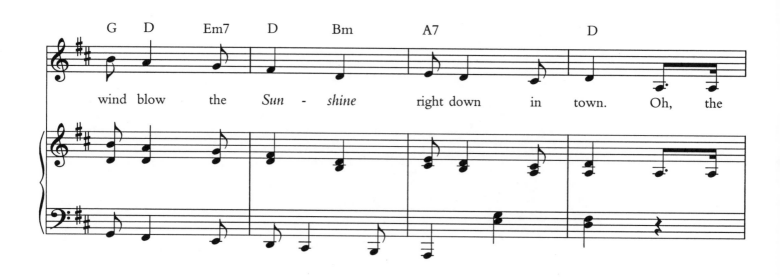

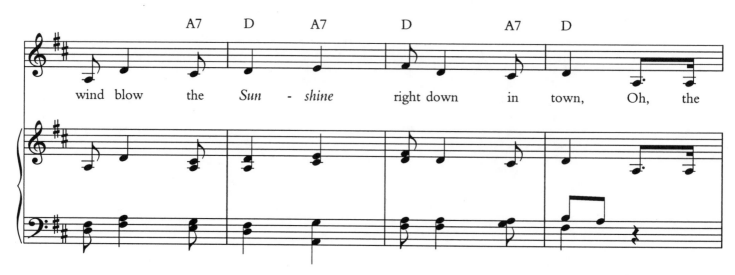

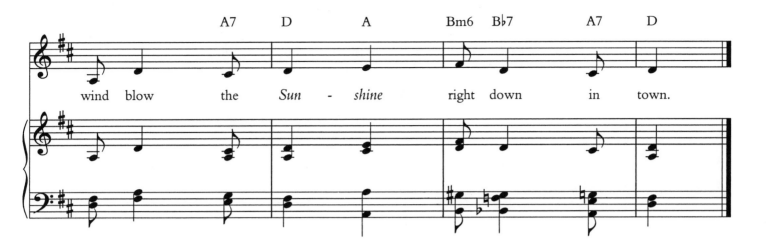

Oh, the wind blow east,
The wind blow west,
The wind blow the *Setting Star*
Right down in town.
    Oh, the wind blow the *Setting Star* right down in town.
    Oh, the wind blow the *Setting Star* right down in town.

Oh, the wind blow east,
The wind blow west,
The wind blow the water
Right down in town.
    Oh, the wind blow the water right down in town.
    Oh, the wind blow the water right down in town.

For children who delight in helping make up songs—and what child does not?—"Riding in the Buggy," a South Carolina play song, is a perfect choice. Children can offer Miss Mary Jane an endless variety of transportation; she can ride in a car, boat, plane, and even on an elephant, camel, or aardvark!

RIDING IN THE BUGGY, MISS MARY JANE

G7   C

Who moan   for   me,   my dar – ling,   who moan   for   me?

D.C. al Fine

A southern schoolgirl acts out a "play-song"—perhaps "Riding in the Buggy, Miss Mary Jane"—around 1910.

An ominous figure from the dark days of slavery, the "pateroller" appears over and over in black song and story. If a plantation overseer discovered a slave missing, he sent for the patrolers ("patrollers," in black dialect), poor whites who made money by hunting down runaways and bringing them back for punishment.

Escaping slaves made their move at night, when the patrolers would be least likely to find them in the woods or swamps. The phrase "it's almost day" suggests good news in Christmas music, but here, it has the ring of a dire threat: dawn means capture. Like many similar songs, however, "Run, Chillen, Run" has been softened by the passage of time. This version describes an exciting chase rather than a terrifying flight through the night.

RUN, CHILLEN, RUN

That child ran, and that child flew, That child lost his Sun - day shoe.

D.C. al Fine

Jumped the fence and ran through the pasture,
First ran slow and then ran faster. *Chorus*

Let me tell you what I'll do,
I'm going to find me a Sunday shoe. *Chorus*

Let me tell you where I'll be,
I'm going to hide behind that tree. *Chorus*

Overflowing with youthful high spirits, a boy speeds through his own version of "Run, Chillen, Run."

Black children who lived along the banks of the Mississippi River used to watch big dredgers scooping up mud and sand to deepen the river's shipping channels. Their observations led to this song, which incorporates not only the sand scraping but the name Liza Jane, a chicken, and a "hump-back mule," all of them popular images in black songs. Shiloh, another name that often pops up as a refrain in black music, was the ancient town near Jerusalem where the Israelites settled when they first entered Caanan.

SCRAPING UP SAND IN THE BOTTOM OF THE SEA

Oh, how I love her, Good-bye, Li - za Jane.

Black those shoes and make them shine,
Shiloh, Shiloh,
Black those shoes and make them shine,
Shiloh, Liza Jane. *Chorus*

Similarly
A hump-back mule I'm bound to ride . . . *Chorus*

Hopped up a chicken and he flew upstairs . . . *Chorus*

Here is our old friend, the rascally but ever-popular cottontail. John the Rabbit had a number of "mighty habits"—such as making off with a gardener's vegetables, as he does here—but he was never a villain to the slaves who invented him, or to children. After all, how could they hate a weak creature who always outwitted the strong and unfailingly got laughs at the master's expense?

OH, JOHN THE RABBIT

Oh, John the Rab - bit, Yes ma'am, Got a might - y hab - it, Yes ma'am. Jump - ing

in my gar - den, Yes ma'am, Cut - ting down my cab - bage, Yes ma'am, My sweet po - ta - toes,

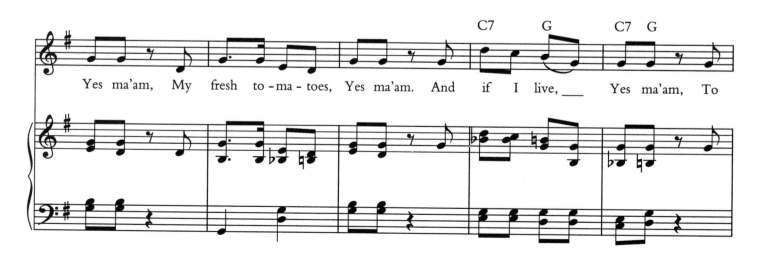

Yes ma'am, My fresh to - ma - toes, Yes ma'am. And if I live, ___ Yes ma'am, To

see next fall, __ Yes ma'am, I ain't gon-na have, _Yes ma'am, No cot-ton at all, Yes ma'am.

Oh, John the Rabbit, Yes ma'am,
Got a mighty habit, Yes ma'am,
Jumping up in the morning, Yes ma'am,

Putting on his clothes, Yes ma'am,
His socks and shoes, Yes ma'am,
His shirt and pants, Yes ma'am,

And if he's ready, Yes ma'am,
By half-past eight, Yes ma'am,
He can go to school, Yes ma'am,
And he won't be late, Yes ma'am.

Like the barnyard, the millpond is a favorite setting for children's songs. For generations, youngsters have enthusiastically sung both "Ducks in the Millpond" and "Go Tell Aunt Rhodie," a tale of death that manages to be amusing, especially to young children. Here are the chorus and one verse of that song:

Go tell Aunt Rhodie,   *She died in the millpond,*
Go tell Aunt Rhodie,   *She died in the millpond,*
Go tell Aunt Rhodie   *She died in the millpond*
The old gray goose is dead.   *From standing on her head.*

DUCKS IN THE MILLPOND

get on a rink - tum, Lord, Lord, _____ gon-na get on a rink - tum.

Ducks in the millpond, a-geese in the clover,
Jumped in the bed, and the bed turned over. *Chorus*

Monkey in the barnyard, a-monkey in the stable,
Monkey get your hair cut as soon as you're able. *Chorus*

Had a little pony, his name was Jack,
I put him in the stable and he jumped through a crack. *Chorus*

Ducks in the millpond, a-geese in the ocean,
A-hug them pretty girls if I take a notion. *Chorus*

Six gleeful friends invite another rider aboard. Mules and other farm animals often show up in
black children's songs.

A play-party song, "Lula Gal" accompanies a children's game in which the participants stand in a circle. One child is chosen to be "it"; in turn, that youngster picks a partner with whom to act out the verses—tie my shoe, comb my hair, and so on. As the game progresses, the performing roles pass from one child to the next until everyone has had a turn in the circle's center.

LULA GAL

Lu - la gal, Lu - la gal, Lu - la gal, Lu - la gal,

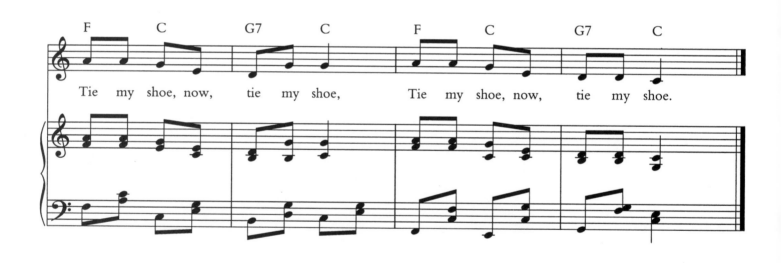

Tie my shoe, now, tie my shoe, Tie my shoe, now, tie my shoe.

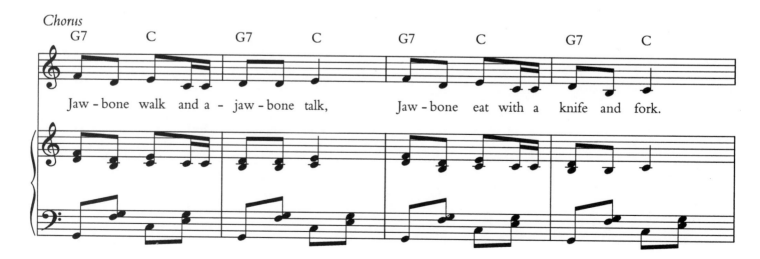

Chorus

Jaw - bone walk and a - jaw - bone talk, Jaw - bone eat with a knife and fork.

Left my jaw-bone in the cor-ner of the fence, And I have not seen my jaw-bone since.

Lula gal, Lula gal,
Lula gal, Lula gal,
Comb my hair now, comb my hair,
Comb my hair now, comb my hair. *Chorus*

Lula gal, Lula gal,
Lula gal, Lula gal,
Hold my hand now, hold my hand,
Hold my hand now, hold my hand. *Chorus*

Lula gal, Lula gal,
Lula gal, Lula gal,
Walk with me now, walk with me,
Walk with me now, walk with me. *Chorus*

The railroad train has long been a powerful symbol in black American music. The train sometimes carries the faithful up to heaven and sometimes takes them to freedom—for a slave, perhaps, interchangeable notions. By extension, then, an oncoming train, its "wheels a-moving and rattling through the land," stands for death itself. A contemporary cantata, "The Lonesome Train," delivers
a moving musical portrait of the cars that brought Abraham Lincoln's body back to Illinois:

> *A lonesome train on a lonesome track,*
> *Seven coaches painted black.*
> *A long train, a quiet train,*
> *Carrying Lincoln home again.*

From "The Lonesome Train," by Earl Robinson and Millard Lampell

LITTLE BLACK TRAIN A-COMING

Oh, the little black train is a-coming,
It's coming 'round the bend,
You can hear those wheels a-moving
And rattling through the land. (2)

Oh, the little black train is a-coming,
It's coming 'round the curve,
A-whistling and a-blowing
And straining every nerve. (2)

A train, the subject of countless black ballads, prepares to carry President Lincoln's body to Illinois in 1865.

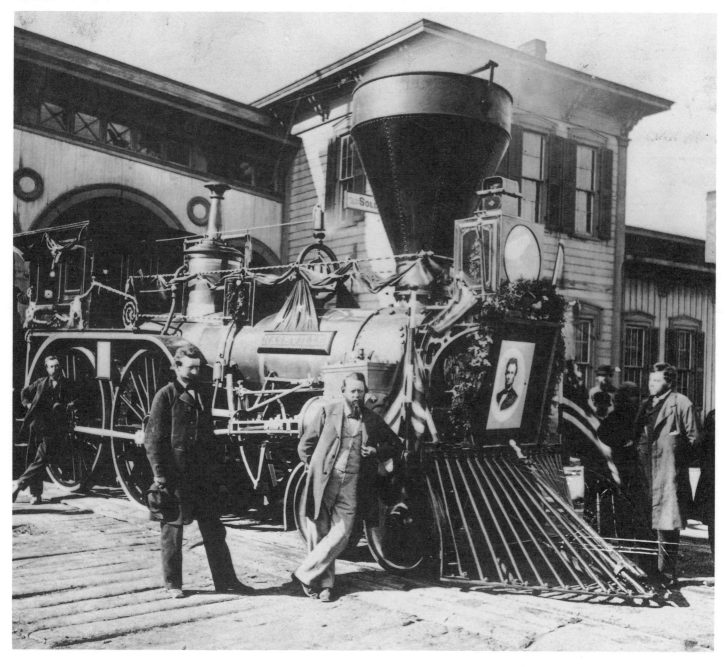

This song dates from slavery, when it was "the preacher [who] went a-hunting." It is sung in the manner of a typical African-American work song, with the leader lining out the story and the group chiming in with the refrain: "Lord, Lord, Lord." The goose, of course, represents the black man, who encounters every imaginable difficulty but still manages to survive. Leadbelly, who recalled singing "The Gray Goose" in a Texas prison, said that he and the other convicts sang the song to express contempt for their white jailers and admiration for the prisoners who stood up to the jailers' cruelties. No matter how solemn the song's origins, however, black children have always regarded it as deliciously funny and have sung it with gales of laughter.

THE GREY GOOSE

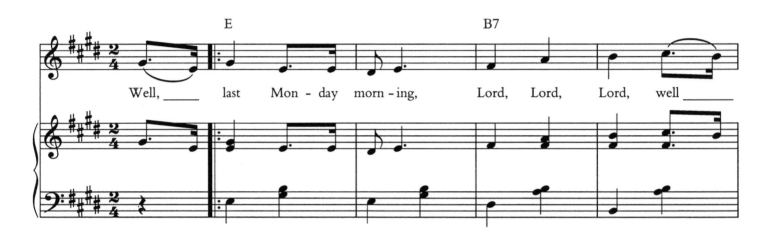

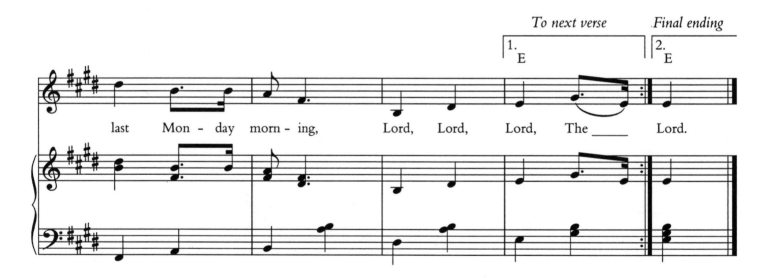

My daddy went a-huntin'. . .
He was huntin' for the grey goose . . .

And he went to the big wood . . .
And he took along his shotgun . . .

Along come a grey goose . . .
Well, he up to his shoulder . . .

And he rammed back the hammer . . .
And he pulled on the trigger . . .

And the shotgun went "boo-loo" . . .
And the shotgun went "boo-loo" . . .

And they put him on a parboil . . .
He was six weeks a-parboil . . .

And they put him on the table . . .
And they put him on the table . . .

And the fork couldn't stick him . . .
And the knife couldn't prick him . . .

Well, they throwed him in the hogpen . . .
And the hogs couldn't eat him . . .

Well, he broke the sow's jawbone . . .
Well, he broke the sow's jawbone . . .

Down he come a-fallin' . . .
He was six weeks a-fallin' . . .

And he put him on the wagon . . .
And he took him to the white house . . .

And your wife and my wife . . .
They give a feather-pickin' . . .

They were six weeks a-pickin' . . .
They were six weeks a-pickin' . . .

So they took him to the sawmill . . .
And he broke the saw's teeth out . . .

And the last time I seen him . . .
And the last time I seen him . . .

He was flyin' 'cross the ocean . . .
Had a long string of goslins . . .

And they all went "Quonk, quonk" . . .
And they all went "Quonk, quonk" . . .

Generations of parents, both black and white, have crooned this lovely, tender lullaby to their little ones. Today's mothers and fathers should learn it and pass it on to their children.

HUSH, LITTLE BABY

Hush lit-tle ba - by, don't say a word, Pa-pa's gon-na buy you a

mock-ing-bird; And if that mock-ing-bird don't sing, Pa-pa's gon-na buy you a dia-mond ring.

And if that diamond ring is brass,
Papa's gonna buy you a looking-glass,
And if that looking-glass gets broke,
Papa's gonna buy you a billy goat.

And if that billy goat don't pull.
Papa's gonna buy you a cart and bull.
And if that cart and bull turn over,
Papa's gonna buy you a dog named Rover.

And if that dog named Rover don't bark,
Papa's gonna buy you a horse and cart.
And if that horse and cart fall down,
You'll still be the sweetest little baby in town.

A teenager's pet billy goat—an animal featured in many black youngsters' songs, including "Hush, Little Baby"—draws mixed reactions from two young observers.